Mighty Machines
CARS

Ian Graham

FIREFLY BOOKS

A FIREFLY BOOK

Published by Firefly Books Ltd. 2010

First printing

Publisher Cataloging-in-Publication Data (U.S.)

Graham, Ian.
    Cars : mighty machines / Ian Graham.
[24] p. : col. photos. ; cm.
Includes index.
Summary: A fun book about cars for young readers, including sports cars, off-road vehicles and racing cars.
ISBN-13: 978-1-55407-627-7 (pbk.)
ISBN-10: 1-55407-627-7 (pbk.)
1. Automobiles – Juvenile literature. I. Title.
[E] 629.222 dc22   TL147.G734 2010

A CIP record for this book is available from Library and Archives Canada

Published in the United States by
Firefly Books (U.S.) Inc.
P.O. Box 1338, Ellicott Station
Buffalo, New York 14205

Published in Canada by
Firefly Books Ltd.
66 Leek Crescent
Richmond Hill, Ontario L4B 1H1

Manufactured by 1010 Printing International Ltd. in Huizhou, Guangdong, China in December 2009, Job #JQ09100342.

Author Ian Graham
Designers Phil and Traci Morash
Editor Paul Manning
Picture Researcher Claudia Tate

Publisher Steve Evans
Creative Director Zeta Davies

Picture credits
Key: t = top, FC = front cover
BMW 4, 14
Corbis George Tiedemann/GT Images 12, Mazen Mahdi/epa 13t, David Cooper/Toronto Star/ZUMA 15t, Don Mason 16, Alex Hofford/epa 20, Brooks Kraft 21t
Getty Images 18
GM UK & Ireland 9t
Rex Paul Cooper FC
Shutterstock Joseph Gareri 5t, Toyota (GB) PLC 6, Richard Foreman 7t, Julie Lucht 8, Anatoliy Meshkov 10, Maserati S.p.A. 11t, Mikolaj Tomczak 17t, Losevsky Pavel 19

Words in **bold** can be found in the glossary on page 23.

Contents

What is a **car**?

The job of a car is to carry us from place to place. Every car has an **engine**. The engine burns **fuel** and provides power to turn the wheels.

trunk

The **trunk** in the back of the car is for carrying things.

A car's engine is a complicated machine with hundreds of moving parts. Slippery oil keeps them all moving easily.

hood

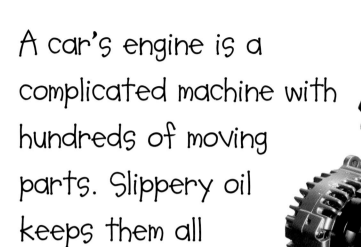

In most cars, the engine is at the front, underneath the **hood**.

Everyday cars

Cars are made in all shapes and sizes. Small cars, or **compacts**, are good for short journeys. Business people who drive long distances prefer bigger cars with more powerful engines.

A car like this would suit a family with two small children.

E 4030 FHP

All cars need fuel.
The bigger the car,
the more fuel it uses.

To save fuel,
this **hybrid** car is
powered by electric
motors as well as a
gasoline engine.

Sports **cars**

Sports cars are designed to be fun to drive. They are small, lightweight, **maneuverable** — and fast!

Some sports cars have a top that can be folded down or taken off completely if the weather is nice. This type of car is called a convertible.

The low, smooth shape of this car helps it to go faster by letting air flow easily over it.

The Chevrolet Corvette has one of the biggest engines of any sports car.

Supercars

Supercars are the most powerful sports cars allowed on the roads. Some supercars have engines so big that they are like two ordinary car engines side by side!

air vent

This Ferrari Enzo has a top speed of 220 miles an hour. Vents at the front and side take in air to cool its massive engine.

The Maserati MC12 is built like a racing car, with the engine behind the driver to better spread the weight.

Supercars are designed to be the best, whatever the cost. Only a few of these amazing cars are ever built.

On the **race track**

Motor racing is one of the most **popular** and exciting sports. All sorts of cars can take part. As well as specially built racing cars, there are races for sports cars and even family cars.

These NASCAR cars are the same shape as ordinary cars, but each is a hand-built racer with a top speed of 200 miles an hour.

Top British driver Lewis Hamilton drives a Formula One racing car.

Formula One racing cars are all single-seaters. They are only half the weight of a family car but are ten times more powerful — that's fast!

In the city

City cars that are used mostly for short journeys do not need to be big and powerful. In fact, the smaller they are, the better!

The Mini is small, but still has space for three **passengers**.

In towns and cities, smaller cars are a lot easier to park. They can squeeze into spaces where bigger cars will not fit.

This city car is so short that it can even be parked sideways.

Carrying more

People carriers, or MPVs (multi-purpose **vehicles**), have more space for passengers than ordinary cars.

The seats of an MPV are raised to give the driver and passengers a better view of the road. The back seats fold down easily to make extra carrying space.

This **mini-MPV** is just the right size and shape for carrying emergency medical supplies.

This roomy MPV has eight seats and still has space for the groceries!

17

Going off-road

When the going gets tough, the car you need is an SUV (Sports Utility Vehicle).

With their chunky tires, SUVs can easily drive over rough or muddy ground without getting stuck. The engine also powers all four wheels, to give more grip on mud, snow and ice.

Only a **four-by-four** could plow through ground as wet and muddy as this!

This Hummer SUV is like the Humvee, the "go-anywhere" patrol car that U.S. Army soldiers drive.

chunky tires

Luxury cars

If you want to travel in real comfort, try a limousine!

Limousines are mostly for important people, such as presidents or kings and queens. But they can be fun to hire for special occasions, such as weddings, too.

The President travels in this specially adapted Cadillac. The body is **armor-plated** and the windows are made of bulletproof glass for protection.

Rolls-Royce is a famous maker of luxury cars.

Extra-long luxury cars are called stretch limos. The longest stretch limos have five doors on each side and seats for up to 10 passengers!

Activities

- What sort of cars are these?

- Draw your own car and make up a story about it. What sort of car is it? Where is it going, and why? Who is traveling in it?

- Make a collection of pictures of different kinds of cars from magazines and comics. How many types can you find?

- If you had to drive along a muddy road, would a sports car or an SUV be better? Which car would you choose, and why?

- Which of these cars would be driven by a racing driver?

Glossary

Armor-plated
Specially strengthened to protect against bullets or missiles.

Compact
A type of car suitable for a small family.

Engine
The machine inside a car that provides power to make the wheels go round.

Four-by-four
A car in which the engine drives all four wheels, not just the two in the front or back.

Fuel
The liquid burned inside a car engine to make it go. Most car engines burn gasoline or diesel.

Hood
The part of a car's body at the front that protects the engine.

Hybrid
A car that saves fuel by using electric motors as well as a gasoline engine to drive the wheels.

Maneuverable
Easy to steer or control.

Mini-MPV
An MPV with fewer seats but a tall space behind for carrying things.

Popular
Liked by a lot of people.

Passengers
The people who travel in a car along with the driver.

Trunk
Space in the back of a car for carrying things.

Vehicle
A machine with an engine that carries people or things.

Index